THIS BOOK BELONGS TO:

CONTACT INFORMATION	
NAME:	
ADDRESS:	
PHONE:	

START / END DATES

_____ / _____ / _____   TO   _____ / _____ / _____

DEDICATION

This Nanny Log Book is dedicated to all the parents out there who want to keep their nanny notes organized and document their findings in the process.

You are my inspiration for producing books and I'm honored to be a part of keeping all of your Nanny notes and records organized.

This journal notebook will help you record the details of your child care records.

Thoughtfully put together with these sections to record: Nanny's Guide, Child Care Info, Daily Log, Special Care, Message for Parents, & Agreement.

HOW TO USE THIS BOOK

The purpose of this book is to keep all of your Child Care notes all in one place. It will help keep you organized.

This Nanny Log Book will allow you to accurately document details about your nanny.

Here are examples of the prompts for you to fill in and write about your experience in this book:

1. Nanny's Guide - Write: Where we will be, Time we will be home, Parent's names, Contact number, Additional Notes, Emergency Contacts,

2. Child Care Information - Record: Child's Name, Age, Meals, Snacks/ Treats, Allergy Info, Favorites (Activity, Game, Toy, Food), Bedtime Routine, Notes.

3. Daily Log - Date, Arrive, Depart, Total Hours, Bathed?, Teeth Brushed?, Diapers (Pee, Poop), Baby's Feedings Schedule (Time of feed, Ounces), Meals (Food Given, Time, Special Instructions & Rules, Nap/ Sleeping Time (Start, End, Total Time), Overall Mood.

4. Special Care - Special Concerns/ Symptoms of Illness, Special Care (Medicine, Time, Dosage, Notes).

5. Message For Parents - For the nanny or babysitter to write a summary of how the time went, any special concerns, supplies needed, etc.

6. Nanny's Agreement Form - Contract agreement including date & day, amount of payment, task list, work schedule, number of children, short term or long term, nanny's signature & date.

NANNY'S GUIDE

WHERE WE WILL BE:	TIME WE WILL BE HOME:

OUR INFORMATION:		CONTACT NUMBER:
MOTHER:		
FATHER:		

ADDITIONAL NOTES:

EMERGENCY CONTACT	
POLICE:	
FIRE:	
DOCTOR:	
DENTIST:	
AMBULANCE:	
OTHERS:	

CHILD CARE INFORMATION

CHILD'S NAME:	AGE:
IN CASE OF EMERGENCY, CALL:	CONTACT #:

MEALS	SNACKS / TREATS

ALLERGIES:

FAVORITES (ACTIVITY, GAME, TOY, FOOD)

BEDTIME ROUTINE

NOTES

DAILY LOG

DATE:		ARRIVE:		DEPART:		TOTAL HOURS:	

BATHED? YES NO	TOOTHBRUSHED? YES NO	TOOTHBRUSHED? YES NO

DIAPERS

TIME	PEE	POOP	NOTES

FEEDINGS

TIME	OUNCES

SPECIAL INSTRUCTIONS FROM MOM:

MEALS

BREAKFAST

TIME:
FOOD GIVEN:

LUNCH

TIME:
FOOD GIVEN:

DINNER

TIME:
FOOD GIVEN:

NAP/SLEEPING TIME

START TIME	END TIME	TOTAL TIME	NOTES

OVERALL MOOD

HAPPY   HYPER   SICK   SAD   PLAYFUL   FUSSY   NEUTRAL

SPECIAL CARE

DATE:		M	T	W	TH	F	SAT	SUN

CONCERNS / SYMPTOMS OF ILLNESS

SPECIAL CARE

TIME	MEDICINE	DOSAGE	NOTES

SPECIAL CONCERNS

MESSAGE FOR PARENTS

DATE:		M	T	W	.TH	F	SAT	SUN

SUPPLIES NEEDED:

O DIAPERS   O WIPES   O BABY FOOD   O FORMULA/MILK   O BATHING SUPPLIES

NANNY'S INITIAL:

NANNY'S AGREEMENT FORM

NAME:	
NUMBER OF CHILD(REN) TO TAKE CARE WITH:	

THIS COMMITMENT IS:	ANTICIPATED DATES
SHORT TERM (LESS THAN 90 DAYS)	
LONG TERM (90 DAYS OR LONGER)	

MY WORK SCHEDULE: O MY WORK SCHEDULE CHANGES

MON	TUE	WED	THU	FRI	SAT	SUN

NANNY'S PROJECTED SCHEDULE:

MON	TUE	WED	THU	FRI	SAT	SUN

PAYMENT:

HOURLY RATE OF	
SALARIED RATE OF PER	
BONUSES	
PAID VACATION DAYS (#)	
PAID HOLIDAYS	

NON-CHILD CARE TASK:

HOUSEWORK
OTHERS (MEAL PREPARATION, PETS, ETC.)

NAME & SIGNATURE	DATE

NANNY'S GUIDE

WHERE WE WILL BE:	TIME WE WILL BE HOME:

OUR INFORMATION:		CONTACT NUMBER:
MOTHER:		
FATHER:		

ADDITIONAL NOTES:

EMERGENCY CONTACT

POLICE:	
FIRE:	
DOCTOR:	
DENTIST:	
AMBULANCE:	
OTHERS:	

CHILD CARE INFORMATION

CHILD'S NAME:	AGE:
IN CASE OF EMERGENCY, CALL:	CONTACT #:

MEALS	SNACKS / TREATS

ALLERGIES:

FAVORITES (ACTIVITY, GAME, TOY, FOOD)

BEDTIME ROUTINE

NOTES

DAILY LOG

DATE:		ARRIVE:		DEPART:		TOTAL HOURS:	

BATHED? YES NO	TOOTHBRUSHED? YES NO	TOOTHBRUSHED? YES NO

DIAPERS

TIME	PEE	POOP	NOTES

FEEDINGS

TIME	OUNCES

SPECIAL INSTRUCTIONS FROM MOM:

MEALS

BREAKFAST

TIME:
FOOD GIVEN:

LUNCH

TIME:
FOOD GIVEN:

DINNER

TIME:
FOOD GIVEN:

NAP/SLEEPING TIME

START TIME	END TIME	TOTAL TIME	NOTES

OVERALL MOOD

HAPPY   HYPER   SICK   SAD   PLAYFUL   FUSSY   NEUTRAL

SPECIAL CARE

DATE: | | M | T | W | TH | F | SAT | SUN

CONCERNS / SYMPTOMS OF ILLNESS

SPECIAL CARE

TIME	MEDICINE	DOSAGE	NOTES

SPECIAL CONCERNS

MESSAGE FOR PARENTS

DATE: | M | T | W | TH | F | SAT | SUN

SUPPLIES NEEDED:

O DIAPERS   O WIPES   O BABY FOOD   O FORMULA/MILK   O BATHING SUPPLIES

NANNY'S INITIAL:

NANNY'S AGREEMENT FORM

NAME:

NUMBER OF CHILD(REN) TO TAKE CARE WITH:

THIS COMMITMENT IS:	ANTICIPATED DATES
SHORT TERM (LESS THAN 90 DAYS)	
LONG TERM (90 DAYS OR LONGER)	

MY WORK SCHEDULE: O MY WORK SCHEDULE CHANGES

MON	TUE	WED	THU	FRI	SAT	SUN

NANNY'S PROJECTED SCHEDULE:

MON	TUE	WED	THU	FRI	SAT	SUN

PAYMENT:

HOURLY RATE OF	
SALARIED RATE OF PER	
BONUSES	
PAID VACATION DAYS (#)	
PAID HOLIDAYS	

NON-CHILD CARE TASK:

HOUSEWORK
OTHERS (MEAL PREPARATION, PETS, ETC.)

NAME & SIGNATURE   DATE

NANNY'S GUIDE

WHERE WE WILL BE:	TIME WE WILL BE HOME:

OUR INFORMATION:		CONTACT NUMBER:
MOTHER:		
FATHER:		

ADDITIONAL NOTES:

EMERGENCY CONTACT

POLICE:	
FIRE:	
DOCTOR:	
DENTIST:	
AMBULANCE:	
OTHERS:	

CHILD CARE INFORMATION

CHILD'S NAME:	AGE:
IN CASE OF EMERGENCY, CALL:	CONTACT #:

MEALS	SNACKS / TREATS

ALLERGIES:

FAVORITES (ACTIVITY, GAME, TOY, FOOD)

BEDTIME ROUTINE

NOTES

DAILY LOG

DATE:		ARRIVE:		DEPART:		TOTAL HOURS:	

BATHED? YES NO	TOOTHBRUSHED? YES NO	TOOTHBRUSHED? YES NO

DIAPERS

TIME	PEE	POOP	NOTES

FEEDINGS

TIME	OUNCES

SPECIAL INSTRUCTIONS FROM MOM:

MEALS

BREAKFAST

TIME:
FOOD GIVEN:

LUNCH

TIME:
FOOD GIVEN:

DINNER

TIME:
FOOD GIVEN:

NAP/SLEEPING TIME

START TIME	END TIME	TOTAL TIME	NOTES

OVERALL MOOD

HAPPY   HYPER   SICK   SAD   PLAYFUL   FUSSY   NEUTRAL

SPECIAL CARE

DATE:		M	T	W	TH	F	SAT	SUN

CONCERNS / SYMPTOMS OF ILLNESS

SPECIAL CARE

TIME	MEDICINE	DOSAGE	NOTES

SPECIAL CONCERNS

MESSAGE FOR PARENTS

DATE: | M | T | W | TH | F | SAT | SUN

SUPPLIES NEEDED:

O DIAPERS   O WIPES   O BABY FOOD   O FORMULA/MILK   O BATHING SUPPLIES

NANNY'S INITIAL:

NANNY'S AGREEMENT FORM

NAME:

NUMBER OF CHILD(REN) TO TAKE CARE WITH:

THIS COMMITMENT IS:	ANTICIPATED DATES
SHORT TERM (LESS THAN 90 DAYS)	
LONG TERM (90 DAYS OR LONGER)	

MY WORK SCHEDULE: O MY WORK SCHEDULE CHANGES

MON	TUE	WED	THU	FRI	SAT	SUN

NANNY'S PROJECTED SCHEDULE:

MON	TUE	WED	THU	FRI	SAT	SUN

PAYMENT:

HOURLY RATE OF	
SALARIED RATE OF PER	
BONUSES	
PAID VACATION DAYS (#)	
PAID HOLIDAYS	

NON-CHILD CARE TASK:

HOUSEWORK
OTHERS (MEAL PREPARATION, PETS, ETC.)

NAME & SIGNATURE   DATE

NANNY'S GUIDE

WHERE WE WILL BE:	TIME WE WILL BE HOME:

OUR INFORMATION:		CONTACT NUMBER:
MOTHER:		
FATHER:		

ADDITIONAL NOTES:

EMERGENCY CONTACT	
POLICE:	
FIRE:	
DOCTOR:	
DENTIST:	
AMBULANCE:	
OTHERS:	

CHILD CARE INFORMATION

CHILD'S NAME:	AGE:
IN CASE OF EMERGENCY, CALL:	CONTACT #:

MEALS	SNACKS / TREATS

ALLERGIES:

FAVORITES (ACTIVITY, GAME, TOY, FOOD)

BEDTIME ROUTINE

NOTES

DAILY LOG

DATE:		ARRIVE:		DEPART:		TOTAL HOURS:	

BATHED? YES NO	TOOTHBRUSHED? YES NO	TOOTHBRUSHED? YES NO

DIAPERS

TIME	PEE	POOP	NOTES

FEEDINGS

TIME	OUNCES

SPECIAL INSTRUCTIONS FROM MOM:

MEALS

BREAKFAST

TIME:
FOOD GIVEN:

LUNCH

TIME:
FOOD GIVEN:

DINNER

TIME:
FOOD GIVEN:

NAP/SLEEPING TIME

START TIME	END TIME	TOTAL TIME	NOTES

OVERALL MOOD

HAPPY   HYPER   SICK   SAD   PLAYFUL   FUSSY   NEUTRAL

SPECIAL CARE

DATE:		M	T	W	TH	F	SAT	SUN

CONCERNS / SYMPTOMS OF ILLNESS

SPECIAL CARE

TIME	MEDICINE	DOSAGE	NOTES

SPECIAL CONCERNS

MESSAGE FOR PARENTS

DATE:		M	T	W	TH	F	SAT	SUN

SUPPLIES NEEDED:

O DIAPERS   O WIPES   O BABY FOOD   O FORMULA/MILK   O BATHING SUPPLIES

NANNY'S INITIAL:

NANNY'S AGREEMENT FORM

NAME:

NUMBER OF CHILD(REN) TO TAKE CARE WITH:

THIS COMMITMENT IS:	ANTICIPATED DATES
SHORT TERM (LESS THAN 90 DAYS)	
LONG TERM (90 DAYS OR LONGER)	

MY WORK SCHEDULE: O MY WORK SCHEDULE CHANGES

MON	TUE	WED	THU	FRI	SAT	SUN

NANNY'S PROJECTED SCHEDULE:

MON	TUE	WED	THU	FRI	SAT	SUN

PAYMENT:

HOURLY RATE OF	
SALARIED RATE OF PER	
BONUSES	
PAID VACATION DAYS (#)	
PAID HOLIDAYS	

NON-CHILD CARE TASK:

HOUSEWORK
OTHERS (MEAL PREPARATION, PETS, ETC.)

NAME & SIGNATURE   DATE

NANNY'S GUIDE

WHERE WE WILL BE:	TIME WE WILL BE HOME:

OUR INFORMATION:		CONTACT NUMBER:
MOTHER:		
FATHER:		

ADDITIONAL NOTES:

EMERGENCY CONTACT	
POLICE:	
FIRE:	
DOCTOR:	
DENTIST:	
AMBULANCE:	
OTHERS:	

CHILD CARE INFORMATION

CHILD'S NAME:	AGE:
IN CASE OF EMERGENCY, CALL:	CONTACT #:

MEALS	SNACKS / TREATS

ALLERGIES:

FAVORITES (ACTIVITY, GAME, TOY, FOOD)

BEDTIME ROUTINE

NOTES

DAILY LOG

DATE:		ARRIVE:		DEPART:		TOTAL HOURS:	

BATHED? YES NO	TOOTHBRUSHED? YES NO	TOOTHBRUSHED? YES NO

DIAPERS

TIME	PEE	POOP	NOTES

FEEDINGS

TIME	OUNCES

SPECIAL INSTRUCTIONS FROM MOM:

MEALS

BREAKFAST

TIME:
FOOD GIVEN:

LUNCH

TIME:
FOOD GIVEN:

DINNER

TIME:
FOOD GIVEN:

NAP/SLEEPING TIME

START TIME	END TIME	TOTAL TIME	NOTES

OVERALL MOOD

HAPPY   HYPER   SICK   SAD   PLAYFUL   FUSSY   NEUTRAL

SPECIAL CARE

DATE: | | M | T | W | TH | F | SAT | SUN

CONCERNS / SYMPTOMS OF ILLNESS

SPECIAL CARE

TIME	MEDICINE	DOSAGE	NOTES

SPECIAL CONCERNS

MESSAGE FOR PARENTS

DATE: | M | T | W | TH | F | SAT | SUN

SUPPLIES NEEDED:

O DIAPERS   O WIPES   O BABY FOOD   O FORMULA/MILK   O BATHING SUPPLIES

NANNY'S INITIAL:

NANNY'S AGREEMENT FORM

NAME:	
NUMBER OF CHILD(REN) TO TAKE CARE WITH:	

THIS COMMITMENT IS:	ANTICIPATED DATES
SHORT TERM (LESS THAN 90 DAYS)	
LONG TERM (90 DAYS OR LONGER)	

MY WORK SCHEDULE: O MY WORK SCHEDULE CHANGES

MON	TUE	WED	THU	FRI	SAT	SUN

NANNY'S PROJECTED SCHEDULE:

MON	TUE	WED	THU	FRI	SAT	SUN

PAYMENT:

HOURLY RATE OF	
SALARIED RATE OF PER	
BONUSES	
PAID VACATION DAYS (#)	
PAID HOLIDAYS	

NON-CHILD CARE TASK:

HOUSEWORK
OTHERS (MEAL PREPARATION, PETS, ETC.)

NAME & SIGNATURE   DATE

NANNY'S GUIDE

WHERE WE WILL BE:	TIME WE WILL BE HOME:

OUR INFORMATION:		CONTACT NUMBER:
MOTHER:		
FATHER:		

ADDITIONAL NOTES:

EMERGENCY CONTACT

POLICE:	
FIRE:	
DOCTOR:	
DENTIST:	
AMBULANCE:	
OTHERS:	

CHILD CARE INFORMATION

CHILD'S NAME:	AGE:
IN CASE OF EMERGENCY, CALL:	CONTACT #:

MEALS	SNACKS / TREATS

ALLERGIES:

FAVORITES (ACTIVITY, GAME, TOY, FOOD)

BEDTIME ROUTINE

NOTES

DAILY LOG

DATE:	ARRIVE:	DEPART:	TOTAL HOURS:

BATHED? YES NO	TOOTHBRUSHED? YES NO	TOOTHBRUSHED? YES NO

DIAPERS

TIME	PEE	POOP	NOTES

FEEDINGS

TIME	OUNCES

SPECIAL INSTRUCTIONS FROM MOM:

MEALS

BREAKFAST

TIME:
FOOD GIVEN:

LUNCH

TIME:
FOOD GIVEN:

DINNER

TIME:
FOOD GIVEN:

NAP/SLEEPING TIME

START TIME	END TIME	TOTAL TIME	NOTES

OVERALL MOOD

HAPPY   HYPER   SICK   SAD   PLAYFUL   FUSSY   NEUTRAL

SPECIAL CARE

DATE: | | M | T | W | TH | F | SAT | SUN

CONCERNS / SYMPTOMS OF ILLNESS

SPECIAL CARE

TIME	MEDICINE	DOSAGE	NOTES

SPECIAL CONCERNS

MESSAGE FOR PARENTS

DATE:		M	T	W	TH	F	SAT	SUN

SUPPLIES NEEDED:

O DIAPERS   O WIPES   O BABY FOOD   O FORMULA/MILK   O BATHING SUPPLIES

NANNY'S INITIAL:

NANNY'S AGREEMENT FORM

NAME:

NUMBER OF CHILD(REN) TO TAKE CARE WITH:

THIS COMMITMENT IS:	ANTICIPATED DATES
SHORT TERM (LESS THAN 90 DAYS)	
LONG TERM (90 DAYS OR LONGER)	

MY WORK SCHEDULE: O MY WORK SCHEDULE CHANGES

MON	TUE	WED	THU	FRI	SAT	SUN

NANNY'S PROJECTED SCHEDULE:

MON	TUE	WED	THU	FRI	SAT	SUN

PAYMENT:

HOURLY RATE OF	
SALARIED RATE OF PER	
BONUSES	
PAID VACATION DAYS (#)	
PAID HOLIDAYS	

NON-CHILD CARE TASK:

HOUSEWORK
OTHERS (MEAL PREPARATION, PETS, ETC.)

NAME & SIGNATURE   DATE

NANNY'S GUIDE

WHERE WE WILL BE:	TIME WE WILL BE HOME:

OUR INFORMATION:		CONTACT NUMBER:
MOTHER:		
FATHER:		

ADDITIONAL NOTES:

EMERGENCY CONTACT	
POLICE:	
FIRE:	
DOCTOR:	
DENTIST:	
AMBULANCE:	
OTHERS:	

CHILD CARE INFORMATION

CHILD'S NAME:	AGE:
IN CASE OF EMERGENCY, CALL:	CONTACT #:

MEALS	SNACKS / TREATS

ALLERGIES:

FAVORITES (ACTIVITY, GAME, TOY, FOOD)

BEDTIME ROUTINE

NOTES

DAILY LOG

DATE:		ARRIVE:		DEPART:		TOTAL HOURS:	

BATHED? YES NO	TOOTHBRUSHED? YES NO	TOOTHBRUSHED? YES NO

DIAPERS

TIME	PEE	POOP	NOTES

FEEDINGS

TIME	OUNCES

SPECIAL INSTRUCTIONS FROM MOM:

MEALS

BREAKFAST

TIME:
FOOD GIVEN:

LUNCH

TIME:
FOOD GIVEN:

DINNER

TIME:
FOOD GIVEN:

NAP/SLEEPING TIME

START TIME	END TIME	TOTAL TIME	NOTES

OVERALL MOOD

HAPPY   HYPER   SICK   SAD   PLAYFUL   FUSSY   NEUTRAL

SPECIAL CARE

DATE: | M | T | W | TH | F | SAT | SUN

CONCERNS / SYMPTOMS OF ILLNESS

SPECIAL CARE

TIME	MEDICINE	DOSAGE	NOTES

SPECIAL CONCERNS

MESSAGE FOR PARENTS

DATE: | M | T | W | TH | F | SAT | SUN

SUPPLIES NEEDED:

O DIAPERS   O WIPES   O BABY FOOD   O FORMULA/MILK   O BATHING SUPPLIES

NANNY'S INITIAL:

NANNY'S AGREEMENT FORM

NAME:

NUMBER OF CHILD(REN) TO TAKE CARE WITH:

THIS COMMITMENT IS:	ANTICIPATED DATES
SHORT TERM (LESS THAN 90 DAYS)	
LONG TERM (90 DAYS OR LONGER)	

MY WORK SCHEDULE: O MY WORK SCHEDULE CHANGES

MON	TUE	WED	THU	FRI	SAT	SUN

NANNY'S PROJECTED SCHEDULE:

MON	TUE	WED	THU	FRI	SAT	SUN

PAYMENT:

HOURLY RATE OF	
SALARIED RATE OF PER	
BONUSES	
PAID VACATION DAYS (#)	
PAID HOLIDAYS	

NON-CHILD CARE TASK:

HOUSEWORK
OTHERS (MEAL PREPARATION, PETS, ETC.)

NAME & SIGNATURE   DATE

NANNY'S GUIDE

WHERE WE WILL BE:	TIME WE WILL BE HOME:

OUR INFORMATION:		CONTACT NUMBER:
MOTHER:		
FATHER:		

ADDITIONAL NOTES:

EMERGENCY CONTACT

POLICE:	
FIRE:	
DOCTOR:	
DENTIST:	
AMBULANCE:	
OTHERS:	

CHILD CARE INFORMATION

CHILD'S NAME:	AGE:
IN CASE OF EMERGENCY, CALL:	CONTACT #:

MEALS	SNACKS / TREATS

ALLERGIES:

FAVORITES (ACTIVITY, GAME, TOY, FOOD)

BEDTIME ROUTINE

NOTES

DAILY LOG

DATE:		ARRIVE:		DEPART:		TOTAL HOURS:	

BATHED? YES NO	TOOTHBRUSHED? YES NO	TOOTHBRUSHED? YES NO

DIAPERS

TIME	PEE	POOP	NOTES

FEEDINGS

TIME	OUNCES

SPECIAL INSTRUCTIONS FROM MOM:

MEALS

BREAKFAST

TIME:
FOOD GIVEN:

LUNCH

TIME:
FOOD GIVEN:

DINNER

TIME:
FOOD GIVEN:

NAP/SLEEPING TIME

START TIME	END TIME	TOTAL TIME	NOTES

OVERALL MOOD

HAPPY   HYPER   SICK   SAD   PLAYFUL   FUSSY   NEUTRAL

SPECIAL CARE

DATE: | M | T | W | TH | F | SAT | SUN

CONCERNS / SYMPTOMS OF ILLNESS

SPECIAL CARE

TIME	MEDICINE	DOSAGE	NOTES

SPECIAL CONCERNS

MESSAGE FOR PARENTS

DATE:		M	T	W	TH	F	SAT	SUN

SUPPLIES NEEDED:

O DIAPERS   O WIPES   O BABY FOOD   O FORMULA/MILK   O BATHING SUPPLIES

NANNY'S INITIAL:

NANNY'S AGREEMENT FORM

NAME:

NUMBER OF CHILD(REN) TO TAKE CARE WITH:

THIS COMMITMENT IS:	ANTICIPATED DATES
SHORT TERM (LESS THAN 90 DAYS)	
LONG TERM (90 DAYS OR LONGER)	

MY WORK SCHEDULE:

O MY WORK SCHEDULE CHANGES

MON	TUE	WED	THU	FRI	SAT	SUN

NANNY'S PROJECTED SCHEDULE:

MON	TUE	WED	THU	FRI	SAT	SUN

PAYMENT:

HOURLY RATE OF	
SALARIED RATE OF PER	
BONUSES	
PAID VACATION DAYS (#)	
PAID HOLIDAYS	

NON-CHILD CARE TASK:

HOUSEWORK
OTHERS (MEAL PREPARATION, PETS, ETC.)

_____
NAME & SIGNATURE

_____
DATE

NANNY'S GUIDE

WHERE WE WILL BE:	TIME WE WILL BE HOME:

OUR INFORMATION:		CONTACT NUMBER:
MOTHER:		
FATHER:		

ADDITIONAL NOTES:

EMERGENCY CONTACT

POLICE:	
FIRE:	
DOCTOR:	
DENTIST:	
AMBULANCE:	
OTHERS:	

CHILD CARE INFORMATION

CHILD'S NAME:	AGE:
IN CASE OF EMERGENCY, CALL:	CONTACT #:

MEALS	SNACKS / TREATS

ALLERGIES:

FAVORITES (ACTIVITY, GAME, TOY, FOOD)

BEDTIME ROUTINE

NOTES

DAILY LOG

DATE:		ARRIVE:		DEPART:		TOTAL HOURS:	

BATHED? YES NO	TOOTHBRUSHED? YES NO	TOOTHBRUSHED? YES NO

DIAPERS

TIME	PEE	POOP	NOTES

FEEDINGS

TIME	OUNCES

SPECIAL INSTRUCTIONS FROM MOM:

MEALS

BREAKFAST

TIME:
FOOD GIVEN:

LUNCH

TIME:
FOOD GIVEN:

DINNER

TIME:
FOOD GIVEN:

NAP/SLEEPING TIME

START TIME	END TIME	TOTAL TIME	NOTES

OVERALL MOOD

HAPPY   HYPER   SICK   SAD   PLAYFUL   FUSSY   NEUTRAL

SPECIAL CARE

DATE: | | M | T | W | TH | F | SAT | SUN

CONCERNS / SYMPTOMS OF ILLNESS

SPECIAL CARE

TIME	MEDICINE	DOSAGE	NOTES

SPECIAL CONCERNS

MESSAGE FOR PARENTS

DATE:		M	T	W	TH	F	SAT	SUN

SUPPLIES NEEDED:

O DIAPERS   O WIPES   O BABY FOOD   O FORMULA/MILK   O BATHING SUPPLIES

NANNY'S INITIAL:

NANNY'S AGREEMENT FORM

NAME:

NUMBER OF CHILD(REN) TO TAKE CARE WITH:

THIS COMMITMENT IS:	ANTICIPATED DATES
SHORT TERM (LESS THAN 90 DAYS)	
LONG TERM (90 DAYS OR LONGER)	

MY WORK SCHEDULE: O MY WORK SCHEDULE CHANGES

MON	TUE	WED	THU	FRI	SAT	SUN

NANNY'S PROJECTED SCHEDULE:

MON	TUE	WED	THU	FRI	SAT	SUN

PAYMENT:

HOURLY RATE OF	
SALARIED RATE OF PER	
BONUSES	
PAID VACATION DAYS (#)	
PAID HOLIDAYS	

NON-CHILD CARE TASK:

HOUSEWORK
OTHERS (MEAL PREPARATION, PETS, ETC.)

NAME & SIGNATURE   DATE

NANNY'S GUIDE

WHERE WE WILL BE:	TIME WE WILL BE HOME:

OUR INFORMATION:	CONTACT NUMBER:
MOTHER:	
FATHER:	

ADDITIONAL NOTES:

EMERGENCY CONTACT

POLICE:	
FIRE:	
DOCTOR:	
DENTIST:	
AMBULANCE:	
OTHERS:	

CHILD CARE INFORMATION

CHILD'S NAME:	AGE:
IN CASE OF EMERGENCY, CALL:	CONTACT #:

MEALS	SNACKS / TREATS

ALLERGIES:

FAVORITES (ACTIVITY, GAME, TOY, FOOD)

BEDTIME ROUTINE

NOTES

DAILY LOG

DATE:		ARRIVE:		DEPART:		TOTAL HOURS:	

BATHED? YES NO	TOOTHBRUSHED? YES NO	TOOTHBRUSHED? YES NO

DIAPERS

TIME	PEE	POOP	NOTES

FEEDINGS

TIME	OUNCES

SPECIAL INSTRUCTIONS FROM MOM:

MEALS

BREAKFAST

TIME:
FOOD GIVEN:

LUNCH

TIME:
FOOD GIVEN:

DINNER

TIME:
FOOD GIVEN:

NAP/SLEEPING TIME

START TIME	END TIME	TOTAL TIME	NOTES

OVERALL MOOD

HAPPY   HYPER   SICK   SAD   PLAYFUL   FUSSY   NEUTRAL

SPECIAL CARE

DATE:		M	T	W	TH	F	SAT	SUN

CONCERNS / SYMPTOMS OF ILLNESS

SPECIAL CARE

TIME	MEDICINE	DOSAGE	NOTES

SPECIAL CONCERNS

MESSAGE FOR PARENTS

DATE:		M	T	W	TH	F	SAT	SUN

SUPPLIES NEEDED:

O DIAPERS   O WIPES   O BABY FOOD   O FORMULA/MILK   O BATHING SUPPLIES

NANNY'S INITIAL:

NANNY'S AGREEMENT FORM

NAME:

NUMBER OF CHILD(REN) TO TAKE CARE WITH:

THIS COMMITMENT IS:	ANTICIPATED DATES
SHORT TERM (LESS THAN 90 DAYS)	
LONG TERM (90 DAYS OR LONGER)	

MY WORK SCHEDULE: O MY WORK SCHEDULE CHANGES

MON	TUE	WED	THU	FRI	SAT	SUN

NANNY'S PROJECTED SCHEDULE:

MON	TUE	WED	THU	FRI	SAT	SUN

PAYMENT:

HOURLY RATE OF	
SALARIED RATE OF PER	
BONUSES	
PAID VACATION DAYS (#)	
PAID HOLIDAYS	

NON-CHILD CARE TASK:

HOUSEWORK
OTHERS (MEAL PREPARATION, PETS, ETC.)

NAME & SIGNATURE   DATE

NANNY'S GUIDE

WHERE WE WILL BE:	TIME WE WILL BE HOME:

OUR INFORMATION:	CONTACT NUMBER:
MOTHER:	
FATHER:	

ADDITIONAL NOTES:

EMERGENCY CONTACT

POLICE:	
FIRE:	
DOCTOR:	
DENTIST:	
AMBULANCE:	
OTHERS:	

CHILD CARE INFORMATION

CHILD'S NAME:

AGE:

IN CASE OF EMERGENCY, CALL:

CONTACT #:

MEALS

SNACKS / TREATS

ALLERGIES:

FAVORITES (ACTIVITY, GAME, TOY, FOOD)

BEDTIME ROUTINE

NOTES

DAILY LOG

DATE:		ARRIVE:		DEPART:		TOTAL HOURS:	

BATHED? YES NO	TOOTHBRUSHED? YES NO	TOOTHBRUSHED? YES NO

DIAPERS

TIME	PEE	POOP	NOTES

FEEDINGS

TIME	OUNCES

SPECIAL INSTRUCTIONS FROM MOM:

MEALS

BREAKFAST

TIME:
FOOD GIVEN:

LUNCH

TIME:
FOOD GIVEN:

DINNER

TIME:
FOOD GIVEN:

NAP/SLEEPING TIME

START TIME	END TIME	TOTAL TIME	NOTES

OVERALL MOOD

HAPPY   HYPER   SICK   SAD   PLAYFUL   FUSSY   NEUTRAL

SPECIAL CARE

DATE: | M | T | W | TH | F | SAT | SUN |

CONCERNS / SYMPTOMS OF ILLNESS

SPECIAL CARE

TIME	MEDICINE	DOSAGE	NOTES

SPECIAL CONCERNS

MESSAGE FOR PARENTS

DATE: | M | T | W | TH | F | SAT | SUN

SUPPLIES NEEDED:

O DIAPERS   O WIPES   O BABY FOOD   O FORMULA/MILK   O BATHING SUPPLIES

NANNY'S INITIAL:

NANNY'S AGREEMENT FORM

NAME:

NUMBER OF CHILD(REN) TO TAKE CARE WITH:

THIS COMMITMENT IS:	ANTICIPATED DATES
SHORT TERM (LESS THAN 90 DAYS)	
LONG TERM (90 DAYS OR LONGER)	

MY WORK SCHEDULE: O MY WORK SCHEDULE CHANGES

MON	TUE	WED	THU	FRI	SAT	SUN

NANNY'S PROJECTED SCHEDULE:

MON	TUE	WED	THU	FRI	SAT	SUN

PAYMENT: ## NON-CHILD CARE TASK:

HOURLY RATE OF		HOUSEWORK	
SALARIED RATE OF PER			
BONUSES		OTHERS (MEAL PREPARATION, PETS, ETC.)	
PAID VACATION DAYS (#)			
PAID HOLIDAYS			

NAME & SIGNATURE   DATE

NANNY'S GUIDE

WHERE WE WILL BE:	TIME WE WILL BE HOME:

OUR INFORMATION:		CONTACT NUMBER:
MOTHER:		
FATHER:		

ADDITIONAL NOTES:

EMERGENCY CONTACT

POLICE:	
FIRE:	
DOCTOR:	
DENTIST:	
AMBULANCE:	
OTHERS:	

CHILD CARE INFORMATION

CHILD'S NAME:

AGE:

IN CASE OF EMERGENCY, CALL:

CONTACT #:

MEALS

SNACKS / TREATS

ALLERGIES:

FAVORITES (ACTIVITY, GAME, TOY, FOOD)

BEDTIME ROUTINE

NOTES

DAILY LOG

DATE:	ARRIVE:	DEPART:	TOTAL HOURS:

BATHED? YES NO	TOOTHBRUSHED? YES NO	TOOTHBRUSHED? YES NO

DIAPERS

TIME	PEE	POOP	NOTES

FEEDINGS

TIME	OUNCES

SPECIAL INSTRUCTIONS FROM MOM:

MEALS

BREAKFAST

TIME:
FOOD GIVEN:

LUNCH

TIME:
FOOD GIVEN:

DINNER

TIME:
FOOD GIVEN:

NAP/SLEEPING TIME

START TIME	END TIME	TOTAL TIME	NOTES

OVERALL MOOD

HAPPY   HYPER   SICK   SAD   PLAYFUL   FUSSY   NEUTRAL

SPECIAL CARE

| DATE: | | M | T | W | TH | F | SAT | SUN |

CONCERNS / SYMPTOMS OF ILLNESS

SPECIAL CARE

TIME	MEDICINE	DOSAGE	NOTES

SPECIAL CONCERNS

MESSAGE FOR PARENTS

DATE:

M	T	W	TH	F	SAT	SUN

SUPPLIES NEEDED:

O DIAPERS   O WIPES   O BABY FOOD   O FORMULA/MILK   O BATHING SUPPLIES

NANNY'S INITIAL:

NANNY'S AGREEMENT FORM

NAME:

NUMBER OF CHILD(REN) TO TAKE CARE WITH:

THIS COMMITMENT IS:	ANTICIPATED DATES
SHORT TERM (LESS THAN 90 DAYS)	
LONG TERM (90 DAYS OR LONGER)	

MY WORK SCHEDULE: O MY WORK SCHEDULE CHANGES

MON	TUE	WED	THU	FRI	SAT	SUN

NANNY'S PROJECTED SCHEDULE:

MON	TUE	WED	THU	FRI	SAT	SUN

PAYMENT:

HOURLY RATE OF	
SALARIED RATE OF PER	
BONUSES	
PAID VACATION DAYS (#)	
PAID HOLIDAYS	

NON-CHILD CARE TASK:

HOUSEWORK
OTHERS (MEAL PREPARATION, PETS, ETC.)

NAME & SIGNATURE   DATE

NANNY'S GUIDE

WHERE WE WILL BE:	TIME WE WILL BE HOME:

OUR INFORMATION:		CONTACT NUMBER:
MOTHER:		
FATHER:		

ADDITIONAL NOTES:

EMERGENCY CONTACT

POLICE:	
FIRE:	
DOCTOR:	
DENTIST:	
AMBULANCE:	
OTHERS:	

CHILD CARE INFORMATION

CHILD'S NAME:	AGE:
IN CASE OF EMERGENCY, CALL:	CONTACT #:

MEALS	SNACKS / TREATS

ALLERGIES:

FAVORITES (ACTIVITY, GAME, TOY, FOOD)

BEDTIME ROUTINE

NOTES

DAILY LOG

DATE:		ARRIVE:		DEPART:		TOTAL HOURS:	

BATHED? YES NO	TOOTHBRUSHED? YES NO	TOOTHBRUSHED? YES NO

DIAPERS

TIME	PEE	POOP	NOTES

FEEDINGS

TIME	OUNCES

SPECIAL INSTRUCTIONS FROM MOM:

MEALS

BREAKFAST

TIME:
FOOD GIVEN:

LUNCH

TIME:
FOOD GIVEN:

DINNER

TIME:
FOOD GIVEN:

NAP/SLEEPING TIME

START TIME	END TIME	TOTAL TIME	NOTES

OVERALL MOOD

HAPPY   HYPER   SICK   SAD   PLAYFUL   FUSSY   NEUTRAL

SPECIAL CARE

| DATE: | | M | T | W | TH | F | SAT | SUN |

CONCERNS / SYMPTOMS OF ILLNESS

SPECIAL CARE

TIME	MEDICINE	DOSAGE	NOTES

SPECIAL CONCERNS

MESSAGE FOR PARENTS

DATE: | M | T | W | TH | F | SAT | SUN

SUPPLIES NEEDED:

O DIAPERS   O WIPES   O BABY FOOD   O FORMULA/MILK   O BATHING SUPPLIES

NANNY'S INITIAL:

NANNY'S AGREEMENT FORM

NAME:

NUMBER OF CHILD(REN) TO TAKE CARE WITH:

THIS COMMITMENT IS:	ANTICIPATED DATES
SHORT TERM (LESS THAN 90 DAYS)	
LONG TERM (90 DAYS OR LONGER)	

MY WORK SCHEDULE: O MY WORK SCHEDULE CHANGES

MON	TUE	WED	THU	FRI	SAT	SUN

NANNY'S PROJECTED SCHEDULE:

MON	TUE	WED	THU	FRI	SAT	SUN

PAYMENT:

HOURLY RATE OF	
SALARIED RATE OF PER	
BONUSES	
PAID VACATION DAYS (#)	
PAID HOLIDAYS	

NON-CHILD CARE TASK:

HOUSEWORK
OTHERS (MEAL PREPARATION, PETS, ETC.)

NAME & SIGNATURE   DATE

NANNY'S GUIDE

WHERE WE WILL BE:	TIME WE WILL BE HOME:

OUR INFORMATION:	CONTACT NUMBER:
MOTHER:	
FATHER:	

ADDITIONAL NOTES:

EMERGENCY CONTACT

POLICE:	
FIRE:	
DOCTOR:	
DENTIST:	
AMBULANCE:	
OTHERS:	

CHILD CARE INFORMATION

CHILD'S NAME:

AGE:

IN CASE OF EMERGENCY, CALL:

CONTACT #:

MEALS	SNACKS / TREATS

ALLERGIES:

FAVORITES (ACTIVITY, GAME, TOY, FOOD)

BEDTIME ROUTINE

NOTES

DAILY LOG

DATE:		ARRIVE:		DEPART:		TOTAL HOURS:	

BATHED? YES NO	TOOTHBRUSHED? YES NO	TOOTHBRUSHED? YES NO

DIAPERS

TIME	PEE	POOP	NOTES

FEEDINGS

TIME	OUNCES

SPECIAL INSTRUCTIONS FROM MOM:

MEALS

BREAKFAST

TIME:
FOOD GIVEN:

LUNCH

TIME:
FOOD GIVEN:

DINNER

TIME:
FOOD GIVEN:

NAP/SLEEPING TIME

START TIME	END TIME	TOTAL TIME	NOTES

OVERALL MOOD

HAPPY   HYPER   SICK   SAD   PLAYFUL   FUSSY   NEUTRAL

SPECIAL CARE

DATE: | | M | T | W | TH | F | SAT | SUN

CONCERNS / SYMPTOMS OF ILLNESS

SPECIAL CARE

TIME	MEDICINE	DOSAGE	NOTES

SPECIAL CONCERNS

MESSAGE FOR PARENTS

DATE:		M	T	W	TH	F	SAT	SUN

SUPPLIES NEEDED:

O DIAPERS   O WIPES   O BABY FOOD   O FORMULA/MILK   O BATHING SUPPLIES

NANNY'S INITIAL:

NANNY'S AGREEMENT FORM

NAME:	
NUMBER OF CHILD(REN) TO TAKE CARE WITH:	

THIS COMMITMENT IS:	ANTICIPATED DATES
SHORT TERM (LESS THAN 90 DAYS)	
LONG TERM (90 DAYS OR LONGER)	

MY WORK SCHEDULE: O MY WORK SCHEDULE CHANGES

MON	TUE	WED	THU	FRI	SAT	SUN

NANNY'S PROJECTED SCHEDULE:

MON	TUE	WED	THU	FRI	SAT	SUN

PAYMENT:

HOURLY RATE OF	
SALARIED RATE OF PER	
BONUSES	
PAID VACATION DAYS (#)	
PAID HOLIDAYS	

NON-CHILD CARE TASK:

HOUSEWORK
OTHERS (MEAL PREPARATION, PETS, ETC.)

NAME & SIGNATURE	DATE

NANNY'S GUIDE

WHERE WE WILL BE:	TIME WE WILL BE HOME:

OUR INFORMATION:		CONTACT NUMBER:
MOTHER:		
FATHER:		

ADDITIONAL NOTES:

EMERGENCY CONTACT

POLICE:	
FIRE:	
DOCTOR:	
DENTIST:	
AMBULANCE:	
OTHERS:	

CHILD CARE INFORMATION

CHILD'S NAME:

AGE:

IN CASE OF EMERGENCY, CALL:

CONTACT #:

MEALS

SNACKS / TREATS

ALLERGIES:

FAVORITES (ACTIVITY, GAME, TOY, FOOD)

BEDTIME ROUTINE

NOTES

DAILY LOG

DATE:		ARRIVE:		DEPART:		TOTAL HOURS:	

BATHED? YES NO	TOOTHBRUSHED? YES NO	TOOTHBRUSHED? YES NO

DIAPERS

TIME	PEE	POOP	NOTES

FEEDINGS

TIME	OUNCES

SPECIAL INSTRUCTIONS FROM MOM:

MEALS

BREAKFAST

TIME:
FOOD GIVEN:

LUNCH

TIME:
FOOD GIVEN:

DINNER

TIME:
FOOD GIVEN:

NAP/SLEEPING TIME

START TIME	END TIME	TOTAL TIME	NOTES

OVERALL MOOD

HAPPY   HYPER   SICK   SAD   PLAYFUL   FUSSY   NEUTRAL

SPECIAL CARE

DATE: | | M | T | W | TH | F | SAT | SUN

CONCERNS / SYMPTOMS OF ILLNESS

SPECIAL CARE

TIME	MEDICINE	DOSAGE	NOTES

SPECIAL CONCERNS

MESSAGE FOR PARENTS

DATE:

M	T	W	TH	F	SAT	SUN

SUPPLIES NEEDED:

O DIAPERS   O WIPES   O BABY FOOD   O FORMULA/MILK   O BATHING SUPPLIES

NANNY'S INITIAL:

NANNY'S AGREEMENT FORM

NAME:	

NUMBER OF CHILD(REN) TO TAKE CARE WITH:	

THIS COMMITMENT IS:	ANTICIPATED DATES
SHORT TERM (LESS THAN 90 DAYS)	
LONG TERM (90 DAYS OR LONGER)	

MY WORK SCHEDULE: O MY WORK SCHEDULE CHANGES

MON	TUE	WED	THU	FRI	SAT	SUN

NANNY'S PROJECTED SCHEDULE:

MON	TUE	WED	THU	FRI	SAT	SUN

PAYMENT: NON-CHILD CARE TASK:

PAYMENT		NON-CHILD CARE TASK	
HOURLY RATE OF		HOUSEWORK	
SALARIED RATE OF PER			
BONUSES		OTHERS (MEAL PREPARATION, PETS, ETC.)	
PAID VACATION DAYS (#)			
PAID HOLIDAYS			

NAME & SIGNATURE	DATE

NANNY'S GUIDE

WHERE WE WILL BE:	TIME WE WILL BE HOME:

OUR INFORMATION:		CONTACT NUMBER:
MOTHER:		
FATHER:		

ADDITIONAL NOTES:

EMERGENCY CONTACT

POLICE:	
FIRE:	
DOCTOR:	
DENTIST:	
AMBULANCE:	
OTHERS:	

CHILD CARE INFORMATION

CHILD'S NAME:

AGE:

IN CASE OF EMERGENCY, CALL:

CONTACT #:

MEALS

SNACKS / TREATS

ALLERGIES:

FAVORITES (ACTIVITY, GAME, TOY, FOOD)

BEDTIME ROUTINE

NOTES

DAILY LOG

DATE:		ARRIVE:		DEPART:		TOTAL HOURS:	

BATHED? YES NO	TOOTHBRUSHED? YES NO	TOOTHBRUSHED? YES NO

DIAPERS

TIME	PEE	POOP	NOTES

FEEDINGS

TIME	OUNCES

SPECIAL INSTRUCTIONS FROM MOM:

MEALS

BREAKFAST

TIME:
FOOD GIVEN:

LUNCH

TIME:
FOOD GIVEN:

DINNER

TIME:
FOOD GIVEN:

NAP/SLEEPING TIME

START TIME	END TIME	TOTAL TIME	NOTES

OVERALL MOOD

HAPPY   HYPER   SICK   SAD   PLAYFUL   FUSSY   NEUTRAL

SPECIAL CARE

DATE:		M	T	W	TH	F	SAT	SUN

CONCERNS / SYMPTOMS OF ILLNESS

SPECIAL CARE

TIME	MEDICINE	DOSAGE	NOTES

SPECIAL CONCERNS

MESSAGE FOR PARENTS

DATE:		M	T	W	TH	F	SAT	SUN

SUPPLIES NEEDED:

O DIAPERS   O WIPES   O BABY FOOD   O FORMULA/MILK   O BATHING SUPPLIES

NANNY'S INITIAL:

NANNY'S AGREEMENT FORM

NAME:

NUMBER OF CHILD(REN) TO TAKE CARE WITH:

THIS COMMITMENT IS:	ANTICIPATED DATES
SHORT TERM (LESS THAN 90 DAYS)	
LONG TERM (90 DAYS OR LONGER)	

MY WORK SCHEDULE: O MY WORK SCHEDULE CHANGES

MON	TUE	WED	THU	FRI	SAT	SUN

NANNY'S PROJECTED SCHEDULE:

MON	TUE	WED	THU	FRI	SAT	SUN

PAYMENT:

HOURLY RATE OF	
SALARIED RATE OF PER	
BONUSES	
PAID VACATION DAYS (#)	
PAID HOLIDAYS	

NON-CHILD CARE TASK:

HOUSEWORK
OTHERS (MEAL PREPARATION, PETS, ETC.)

NAME & SIGNATURE   DATE

www.ingramcontent.com/pod-product-compliance
Lightning Source LLC
Chambersburg PA
CBHW080602030426
42336CB00019B/3293